MW00915938

THE SPIRIT OF MINDFUL DRINKING

Preface

This book is for those who have a love for alcoholic beverages but find that it has developed into an unhealthy relationship. Whether it's a daily occurrence or just a weekend indulgence, if you feel it's too much, this book is for you.

By purchasing this book, you have taken a significant and important step towards establishing a healthier relationship with alcohol.

However, for many individuals, finding a balance with alcohol is not an option. It's crucial to be honest with yourself about this. If you're not honest, this book won't be able to help you. In fact, the only solution that will truly assist you is complete abstinence. And if that is the case, I sincerely recommend for you to get professional help.

If you find yourself in a different situation and need guidance on establishing a healthy relationship with alcohol, this book can assist you in achieving balance without excessive drinking or negatively impacting your life and environment. It offers valuable insights to help you cultivate mindfulness and harmony in your approach to drinking.

Even if you are not a "clinical alcoholic", and you sincerely just want to find more balance and regain control to enjoy Mindful Drinking, it can still be a really good investment for you to seek the help of a professional.

This book started as a therapeutic exercise for me, when journaling during my phase of recovering from an unhealthy relationship with alcohol.

In my younger years I never indulged in excessive alcohol consumption or developed a habit of drinking without socializing. However, as I entered my late 40s,

I found myself engaging in daytime drinking. I would convince myself that it was not excessive, that it was manageable. Yet deep down, I refused to acknowledge that it had become a problem, affecting my relationships, work life, and social interactions. For years, I justified my behavior, sincerely believing that I had control because I could stop at any time. And indeed, I would stop for stretches of a month or even several months, just to proove to myself that I was not dependent.

Today I have a healthy relationship with alcohol. I saved my marriage and the respect of my children. I even found back to friendships that were in a bad place.

In this book, I share the steps I took to achieve this transformation. I offer a comprehensive guide that will help you break free from your toxic relationship with alcohol and find a mindful balance in the way you enjoy a glass of wine or what kind of alcohol you desire.

The first step is to acknowledge that this issue is larger than yourself. Take responsibility for putting yourself in this situation, without placing blame on others. Let go of what it was and what it is. Have faith in what it will be.

With this book in your hand, you have taken the first and most important step towards a better life for yourself and for those who loves you. Embrace that as your first win.

I want to dedicate this book to my therapist that helped and guided me with true dedication and expertise. He is a 14-year sober alcoholic, and he did not believe in me all the way. Not that he wanted to be mean, but because he knows what it takes, and how few manage to get out on the other side. And the truth is, if you don't do this in a certain way, you will not be able to have a mindful relationship with alcohol.

This is bigger than you, and you'll have to accept that.

Introduction to Mindful Drinking

Firstly, it is important to understand the concept of "Mindful Drinking" as it is used in this book. The term refers to a desired relationship with alcohol that is characterized by mindfulness and moderation. Throughout the book, this type of relationship is referred to as a healthy one.

This approach to alcohol consumption involves being conscious and intentional about how much you drink, why you are drinking, and how it makes you feel. It encourages individuals to be aware of their personal limits and make choices that align with their values and well-being.

The decision to buy this book, might be the best decision in your life. The fact that you're reading it is the start for your journey towards mindful drinking—a path that leads not just to healthier habits, but to a deeper understanding of yourself and your relationship with alcohol.

The Essence of Mindful Drinking

At its core, mindful drinking is about intentionality. It's the practice of being fully present with your drinking habits, understanding your motivations, and making conscious choices about when and how much to drink.

Why Mindful Drinking?

The consumption of alcohol is deeply embedded in many cultures around the world, often associated with celebration, socialization, and relaxation. While moderate alcohol consumption can be a part of a balanced lifestyle for many individuals, excessive drinking poses significant risks to both physical health and interpersonal relationships.

Understanding these risks underscores the importance of cultivating a healthy and normal relationship with alcohol.

Health Risks of Excessive Alcohol Consumption

Excessive alcohol consumption can lead to a myriad of health problems, both acute and chronic. On a physical level, heavy drinking is linked to an increased risk of liver diseases, including fatty liver, alcoholic hepatitis, and cirrhosis. It can also contribute to cardiovascular problems, such as hypertension, heart disease, and stroke. The risk of certain cancers, including breast, liver, esophagus, throat, and mouth cancer, is elevated with high alcohol intake.

On a mental health front, alcohol is closely tied to conditions such as depression, anxiety, and increased risk of suicide. Alcohol can affect mood and behavior. This can lead to a vicious cycle where individuals drink to alleviate stress or emotional pain, only to find that alcohol exacerbates these conditions over time.

Beyond health, excessive alcohol consumption can severely impact relationships and social interactions. Alcohol misuse can strain relationships with family, friends, and colleagues.

There are so many reasons to get in control of your alcohol relationship, in fact there is no reasons not to. And it starts with you. Your self-recognition. You must come to terms with the fact that the impetus for change comes from within you, not from external conditions or circumstances. You need to acknowledge, that this is bigger than you.

Once you embrace this understanding, you're ready to embark on the journey toward transformation.

The Importance of a Healthy Relationship with Alcohol

Developing a healthy relationship with alcohol involves recognizing its potential impact on your health and relationships and making informed choices about consumption. Moderation is key.

Health organizations and governments issue recommended limits for alcohol consumption to guide individuals towards safer drinking patterns. Globally, health organizations advocate for moderation in alcohol consumption, echoing a common sentiment for mindful drinking practices. Guidelines typically suggest limits that amount to a specific amount of alcohol per day or week, though specific recommendations may vary by country.

Adhering to these internationally recognized benchmarks can help mitigate the risk of alcohol-related health complications and safeguard the integrity of personal relationships.

The Why?

It's important to be aware of the reasons behind your drinking and to recognize when alcohol might be used as a coping mechanism for underlying issues. Recognizing these underlying issues can help you pinpoint situations to steer clear of or moments to abstain from alcohol consumption, completely.

Ask yourself these questions: What is your why? Are you drinking on emotions? Is there anything in your surrounding environment that affects your behavior around alcohol?

Being mindful about alcohol consumption is not just about avoiding negative consequences; it's about making choices that enhance your overall well-being and quality of life. It's about enjoying alcohol if you choose to drink, without letting it control your health or dictate the quality of your relationships.

By adopting a mindful approach to drinking, you can enjoy the social and cultural aspects of alcohol in a way that respects your body and nurtures your relationships.

This is Mindful Drinking.

The Inward Journey

Let the journey begin.

One of the first things I was asked by my therapist was to abstain from alcohol for a straight 30 days. Throughout this period, I was encouraged to journal my thoughts about alcohol, assess my focus, and above all, reflect on my sources of gratitude.

My first reaction to this was; "I can do this, because I am not an alcoholic, and I'll prove that to him". And I successfully abstained from alcohol for 30 days. Without problems. Because I was decided to do so. But I realized during the 30 days, that this was not the hard part.

What really happened during that period, had nothing to do with me proving anything to him or myself. I knew I could do it, and he probably did, too. But the real gain here, was the clarity and the time to reflect on the endgame. The future me. I had time to delve into who I wanted to be. And let it sink in. The 30 days also provided space to think about the "why" and realize that it was all emanating from within me.

In the passage toward mindful drinking, it's vital to acknowledge an immutable truth: the journey begins and is sustained from within you. This chapter is an exploration of the internal landscape where the heart of change beats, a call to profound self-awareness that never underestimates the gravity of the challenge.

I strongly advise you, to start this journey with 30 days without alcohol. Not to prove anything to you or anyone else regarding your capacity for abstinence. But to give you clarity and time to reflect. Write down your thoughts, and I guarantee you, you'll circle back to those notes many times during the next month's towards your goal.

When you don't have to "look forward" to your next drink or plan an event where it is allowed for you to drink, your focus automatically shifts towards your goal, and that room for reflections will benefit you multiple times the coming months.

It's on you, no one else. Accept it.

Blaming your spouse, boss, sister, kids or anyone is not just a diversion from the truth; it's a relinquishment of your power to change. Personal transformation, especially in your relationship with alcohol, begins and ends with personal responsibility.

But understand this: In grappling with one's relationship with alcohol, the path to transformation extends far beyond acknowledgment of the problem. It's an intimate dance with surrender, an admission that what you face is larger than yourself. This is not a concession of defeat; rather, it's an acceptance that the force of habit – the intricate web of routines, rituals, and reflexes that has been spun over time – possesses a strength and tenacity that cannot be underestimated.

Habits, especially those intertwined with use of alcohol, often operate beyond the realm of conscious thought, laying deep within the bedrock of our daily existence. They are the unseen currents that pull us along, often without our notice. The journey towards change is about unearthing these currents and recognizing their power.

When you surrender to the magnitude of this force, you open yourself to strategic change. It's an approach that respects the potency of ingrained habits and seeks to navigate them with intention over force. This surrender is not an act of passivity but one of active engagement. It's required to initiate true and lasting change.

As such, your surrender to the size and scope of the challenge is not a white flag of surrender but a torchlight parade into the heart of the battle. It's the beginning of a courageous quest to reclaim sovereignty over your choices, your habits, and ultimately, your life.

And you, and only you can truly change your life.

If your life was a movie

You've probably been asked this question before:

If you went and saw "Your Movie" – would you like to see it again?
It's a very legit question, and bear in mind, that you are the author of your own life. No one else, but you. Regularly asking yourself this question ensures that your life's quality aligns with your desires.

Or more importantly – also ask yourself this question; "Are you the star of your own movie, or just an extra?"

These are important questions and I think you know what the answers should be.

If you don't like the answers you get, rewrite the script. What happened in the past, you can't change. But you are definitely in charge of how the movie goes from here.
Take a look at the cast. Are you happy with the crew around you? I strongly suggest you take a really close look at the people surrounding you and cut out all negative people from your life. YES – read it again. If people have a negative attitude, they are no good to you, and you should choose not to have them in your life, and not letting them influence you.

You are the sole director, and the power lies within you to do, have, become anything you want. All it takes is a desire to change and faith that you can do it. Because you can. And you don't need anyone else to do it. Remember; it's all on you. The reason you are where you are, and it's all on you to move to a better place from here.

The Blame Game is a road to nowhere. Blame is a seductive escape, a siren's song that promises relief from the storm of accountability. It whispers that someone else is steering your ship, that the waves battering against your willpower are not of your making. But here's the hard truth: blame is a dead end. Casting it upon others for your drinking habits is akin to handing over the steering wheel of your life to chance winds.

As you take this journey, forgiveness becomes a critical companion. Forgive yourself for past missteps; they do not define your future. Forgive others who may have unwittingly contributed to your struggles with alcohol—not to absolve them, but to free yourself from the anchor of resentment. Forgiveness is not an endorsement of the past; it's an affirmation of your commitment to move forward.

From Victimhood to Victory

Releasing blame is like shedding an old skin. It's uncomfortable, even painful, but it's also a rebirth into empowerment. The victim narrative may have its comforts, but it also has its chains. Breaking free means acknowledging that you have the power to change your narrative, to turn your story from one of helplessness to one of victory. And once you understand that power you can do anything you want.

It doesn't mean you don't need support. Your journey is personal, but you don't have to take it alone. You can seek support from your loved ones, join a support group or a therapist. Or maybe this book can help you accomplish what you want. How you proceed from here is your decision, it's a personal choice and act.

I have experienced blame and victimizing myself. At one time blame was my reflex. A tough day at work meant I deserved a drink. A disagreement at home meant I needed one. This pattern was my escape until I realized that with every sip taken in blame, I surrendered a piece of my freedom.

The journey to mindful drinking began the day I took ownership of my choices, the day I understood that true freedom was not in the glass but in the decision to lift it or leave it.

There's a constructive way to own your journey. It's about rewriting the script, not with self-reproach but with self-respect. It means setting boundaries where needed and communicating openly and honestly about your needs and challenges.

It's acknowledging that while you can't control every circumstance, you can control your response to them.

When you fully surrender to the fact, that it is you, and only you that is responsible for your success and you feel mission accomplished, bear in mind that you are not "done". The Devil will reside in you for a long time, maybe for the rest of your life.

Understand that your self-worth is crucial for success. If you don't have a high sense of self-worth, you will not succeed, because the doubt will haunt you, and trap you in a cycle of scarcity and limitation. You must believe in yourself. On the other hand, having too much self-regard can lead to a sense of disconnection, where you feel too secure of your own success. Remember; this is bigger than you. The Devil will not let you go overnight.

Visualize the Devil perched on your left shoulder. Embrace him not as a foe, but as a constant reminder of the vigilance your journey requires. This symbolic presence embodies the persistent challenges and temptations that will accompany you every step of the way. The devil personifies your old habits and will repeatedly coax you with thoughts like, "Have that 6th drink," "No one will know," or "You can handle it." You may even already recognize some of these voices by now.

Understand that this inner Devil will do whatever it can to get you back to "safety" – your old habits. The sooner you accept the presence of the Devil on your shoulder, the sooner you'll be able to befriend him and eventually turn his presence into a mental tool to ensure that you never grow complacent. It is very important that you don't get into a state of not caring. Respect that there is something bigger than you, and let that Devil sit there to remind you.

And over time, when you are more than acquaintances you might even be some sort of friends and the Devil will know and accept that you win more than you lose, and the new patterns will form, and the Devil will fade.

Recognizing the Red Flags

When you understand and accept, that this originates in you, rather than being influenced by external factors, you gain the ability to identify the red flags and respond appropriately.

The gentle hum of daily life often muffles the internal alarms that signal the beginning of a problematic relationship with alcohol. These early warnings are subtle, easily dismissed by the hustle of responsibilities or drowned in the laughter of another social gathering. However, recognizing these signs is crucial for anyone on the path to mindful drinking. In this chapter, we will identify and learn to heed these signals, understanding that early recognition is the first step towards regaining control and fostering a healthier relationship with alcohol.

Red flags in drinking habits are not always about the quantity consumed; they're often reflective in behavioral changes and shifts in priorities. One of the earliest signals can be a preoccupation with drinking. It starts innocuously—planning for a social event includes thoughts of drinking or perhaps anticipating the evening glass of wine as a reward after a long day. While in moderation, this is not alarming, the red flag waves when these thoughts become persistent, a focal point around which other activities revolve.

Another warning sign is an increasing tolerance to alcohol. What once took a glass or two to feel relaxed now requires more, and you find yourself reaching for that extra drink to achieve the desired effect. This biological signal is a clear indication that your body is adapting to alcohol in ways that can set the stage for increased consumption.

Changes in social habits can also be telling. If you notice that your social activities are increasingly centered around opportunities to drink or if you start to avoid events where alcohol isn't present, it's time to pause and reflect. Similarly, when drinking alone becomes more frequent, and not for the taste or the enjoyment, but for the effect, it's a sign that alcohol is assuming an unhealthy role in your life.

The Emotional Connection

Emotions are closely tied to our behaviors, and alcohol often becomes a salve for stress, anxiety, or depression. When you start using alcohol as a coping mechanism, it's not just a red flag; it's a flare signaling for help. Drinking to numb emotions or escape reality is a dangerous path that can quickly lead to dependency. It's essential to recognize when the drink in your hand is more about emotional management than enjoyment.

The feelings of guilt or shame that follow drinking are equally telling. When the morning brings regrets about the night before, it's not just a hangover—it's a sign that your drinking may not align with your values or the person you want to be. Mindfulness is about being present and at peace with your actions; guilt and shame have no place in that space.

Impact on Daily Life

As drinking becomes problematic, its impact spills into daily life. You may find your performance at work suffering, with concentration lapses or missed deadlines becoming more frequent. Relationships may start to strain under the weight of altered behavior or increased irritability associated with drinking. If loved one's express concern about your drinking habits, it's a significant signal that should not be ignored. The view from the outside can often highlight what you might not see yourself.

Physical health emits crucial signals that demand attention. Alcohol consumption disrupts sleep patterns, leading to insomnia or restless sleep, which may be linked to drinking habits. Additionally, weight gain, unexplained aches, fatigue, skin problems, dark circles under the eyes, and continuous tiredness are ways your body signals a potential issue.

The Denial Dilemma

Denial is the fortress that problematic drinking habits build to protect themselves. It's the voice that tells you *"I can stop anytime I want"* or *"I don't drink any more than my friends do."* This self-deception is a powerful adversary to mindfulness. To overcome it, you must confront your drinking with honesty. Denial thrives on excuses, but self-reflection requires acknowledging the truth of the situation.

To break through denial, start a drinking diary. Track not only how much you drink but also the context and feelings associated with it. This record can be a revealing mirror, reflecting patterns and truths that denial might have masked.

Numerous apps are available to help you track and manage your drinking habits, but what truly resonated with me was journaling. I highly recommend following this advice, being honest with yourself, and committing to it for at least a month. I can assure you that journalizing your drinking patterns will lead to a new perspective on your habits.

To give you a head start on this am happy to share my free journal template– you can download your complimentary copy here.

With a journal in your hand, you create space for self-reflection. Establishing a routine for self-reflection can help in recognizing and addressing these early warning signs. Carve out time each day or week to review your drinking diary and assess your feelings and behaviors.

Ask yourself hard questions: Are you drinking more than you intend to? Are you neglecting responsibilities or relationships in favor of alcohol? How does drinking fit into the life you want to live?

Mindful drinking is not about drastic changes overnight; it's about gradual, intentional shifts in behavior. Use this self-reflection time to set small, achievable goals. Maybe it's about deciding to have alcohol-free days, weeks or months. Or limiting the amount you drink in one sitting. Every small victory in this journey is a step towards a healthier relationship with alcohol.

Awareness is key. Awareness is also learning to listen. The body and mind are adept at sending us messages; the challenge is to listen. Early warning signs are an opportunity, a chance to redirect the course before it's too late. Acknowledging these signals is a brave act, a testament to your strength and commitment to change.

Crafting your personal Drinking Strategy

In this book, I outline the precise steps I took to rebuild a healthy relationship with alcohol. I'm confident that the strategies I implemented will be effective for you too, provided you fully grasp and accept the insights shared. Recognize that the power for change lies within you, and only you have the power to effect that transformation.
I am convinced that the steps and advice forthcoming in these pages will significantly assist you and ultimately lead to the future you earnestly desire.

Acknowledging the necessity of a personal drinking strategy is to accept that mindful drinking is a continuous journey, not a destination. This chapter is dedicated to creating a personal drinking strategy that is not only robust but also flexible, a strategy that you will need to engage with every time alcohol presents itself in your social life.

Understanding that this is a lifetime task will reinforce your commitment to staying on the path of mindful drinking. Below are seven strategic steps to guide you in crafting a drinking strategy that aligns with your values and goals.

In addition to an "overall" strategy, I highly recommend outlining a plan whenever you find yourself in a situation involving alcohol. Personally, I always strategize for social events where I choose to indulge in wine.

My strategies vary based on the specific event. Here are a few examples of successful approaches I've used:

1. Limiting myself to 5 drinks throughout an event, with no more than 1 drink per hour.
2. Enjoying only one glass of wine with friends, then switching to sparkling water in a wine glass.
3. Choosing not to drink. Tell everyone that I am the designated driver.
4. Allowing myself up to 5 glasses of wine during dinner, followed by virgin cocktails. This festive choice goes unnoticed by others, helping me avoid inquiries about why I'm not drinking.

Find your own strategies, and pay attention to what works for you, and re-use the strategies over and over again.

Here are 7 steps to consider before devising your personal drinking strategy:

Step 1: Self-Assessment – Know Your Reasons and Limits

Before devising a strategy, it's essential to understand your current relationship with alcohol. Assess your motivations for drinking: Are they social, emotional, or habitual? Recognize your triggers and your limits.

How much can you drink before it affects your behavior, emotions, and next day's responsibilities? Having a clear view of these aspects is foundational to crafting your strategy.

Step 2: Setting Clear Intentions – The 'Why' Behind Each Drink

Each time you choose to drink, set a clear intention. Why are you choosing to drink at this event? Is it to enjoy the company of friends, to celebrate an occasion, or perhaps to appreciate the craftsmanship of a well-brewed craft beer? Your 'why' should be in harmony with your mindful drinking goals and should not be based on external pressures or to mask emotions.

Step 3: Boundaries – Defining Your Drinking Rules

Create your personal set of drinking rules based on the self-assessment. This might include limits on the number of drinks per occasion, types of alcohol, or even specific days designated as alcohol-free. These rules aren't to restrain but to empower you to enjoy alcohol without compromising your well-being or values. It is important that these rules meet the "public standards" or your governments recommendations as well as your own.

Step 4: Planning – Anticipate and Prepare

Before attending social activities where alcohol will be present, plan your drinking in advance. Decide how many drinks you'll have and what types of drinks you'll choose. Consider the setting and who will be present, and plan for how to handle any pressure to drink more than you intend to.

Step 5: Mindfulness Techniques – Staying Present

Incorporate mindfulness techniques into your drinking strategy. Before taking a sip, take a moment to be present with the drink. Smell it, observe its color and consistency, and take small sips, savoring the flavor. This practice will enhance your enjoyment and help you remain aware of your consumption.

Step 6: Tracking and Adjusting – Keeping Accountable

Keep a record of your drinking: when you drank, how much, and how it made you feel. This log will help you stay accountable and provide insights into patterns that may require adjustment. Be prepared to refine your strategy as needed, based on these reflections.

Step 7: Support Systems – Enlisting Allies

Having a support system is invaluable. Share your strategy with trusted friends or family members who can offer encouragement and help you stick to your plan during social activities. Sometimes, simply knowing someone is there to support your choices can make all the difference.

Crafting Your Strategy

Now, let's delve deeper into crafting your personal drinking strategy. This is not a one-size-fits-all plan but rather a bespoke strategy that fits seamlessly into your life.

Identify Your 'Why'

Start with a mission statement for your drinking. It could be as simple as, "I drink to enhance social experiences, not to escape them." This statement becomes your north star, guiding your decisions about when and how much to drink.

What is your mission statement? Take a moment to reflex and write it down.

My personal advice, which have helped me develop a sustainable strategy:

Know Your Drink

Educate yourself about different types of alcohol and their effects. This knowledge can help you make informed choices about what you consume and how it may impact you. My own personal experience is that "wine is mine". I've found that when I consume stronger spirits like vodka or gin, I struggle to control myself. Therefore, I completely abstain from them.

Additionally, I avoid beer as I value wine as my preferred drink. I prefer not to mix the two due to negative past experiences. You should fine "your spirit", too.

Visualize Success

Before heading to an event, visualize yourself executing your strategy successfully. This mental rehearsal primes you for success and strengthens your resolve.

Take a moment to envision yourself enjoying a delightful evening with friends and family over drinks in a mindful way. Picture immersing yourself in deep and meaningful conversations, making genuine eye contact, sharing laughter effortlessly, and basking in the warmth of others' admiration. Extend this visualization to the next morning, where you wake up with crystal-clear memories of the event, focusing on the often-overlooked small details that make moments special. Recall not just someone's favorite wine, whether it's a crisp Chablis or a rich Chardonnay, but also the heartfelt stories they shared about their loved ones.

Imagine running into one of the attendees later on and effortlessly continuing your conversation by recalling specific details, such as inquiring about their recent brunch adventures or checking on their pet's well-being. If you've ever hesitated to engage in post-event interactions due to a fear of forgetting details, this exercise can empower you to feel more self-assured and connected in social settings.

Visualization is a powerful tool, and it's no surprise that professional athletes often rely on it. There's a good reason for that - it's effective.

Use Discretion

Your drinking strategy is personal. You don't owe anyone an explanation for your choices. If pressed, a simple "I'm good with what I have" is a complete response.

Make it a Habit.

While having a strategy is crucial, rigidity can lead to failure. Life is unpredictable, and even though your strategy should be habitually, don't resort to self-criticism if you deviate from your strategy. Reflect on why and learn from it. Reaffirm your commitment to your strategy and celebrate milestones.

Start over, repeat over and over again until it is a habit.

Celebrate Milestones

Acknowledge and celebrate moments when you successfully follow your strategy, especially in challenging situations. These celebrations reinforce positive behavior and keep you motivated.

No need to say, that celebrations should NOT be a drink, but rather a treat for yourself. A massage, a new piece of clothes you've wanted for a while or perhaps a delicious meal out. Celebrate your success with something you genuinely enjoy and that aligns with your goals.

Remember, drinking is not the only way to have fun or relax. There are countless activities and hobbies that can bring joy, reduce stress, and enhance social connections without relying on alcohol. Explore new interests and prioritize self-care in ways that align with your values and goals.

Conclusion

Crafting your personal drinking strategy is a profound exercise in self-awareness and self-care. By taking the time to develop and commit to your strategy, you are setting yourself up for success in maintaining a mindful relationship with alcohol. Embrace this task as a lifetime commitment to your well-being and remember that every mindful choice is a victory.

Don't overcomplicate your strategy. Keep it simple. Write it down, share it with someone for accountability, but keep it straightforward.

The key to a successful strategy lies in the thoughtful planning process, mental groundwork, and honest self-assessment.

Five Steps Towards Balanced Alcohol Consuption

Achieving a balanced relationship with alcohol is a deeply personal journey, one that takes place within the intricate framework of our habits, emotions, and life experiences.

It's a path that requires accountability, self-compassion, and a steadfast commitment to personal well-being. In this chapter, let's explore 6 fundamental steps to guide you towards balanced alcohol consumption, emphasizing that the transformation you seek is orchestrated by no one but you.

Step 1: Embrace Personal Responsibility

The foundation of balanced drinking is the acceptance of personal responsibility. Recognize that the power to change your drinking habits lies within you. This step is about owning your choices, actions, and ultimately, your journey. Blame is a diversion from the path of balance, a sidestep into victimhood that hinders personal growth.

My experience: In my own journey, the realization that I alone was responsible for my drinking habits was both sobering and empowering. I learned that by taking ownership, I invited a sense of control over my actions and decisions.

Step 2: Cultivate Inner Awareness

Balance begins in the mind. Developing a strong sense of inner awareness allows you to understand your motivations, triggers, and cravings. Engage in daily practices such as meditation or a walk in nature which brings you into the present moment, teaching you to observe your thoughts and feelings without judgment.

My experience: Daily meditation has brought numerous benefits into my life. It provides me with peace, allowing me to delve deep within myself to not only understand my own emotions but also to identify their underlying causes. It also helps me stay focused on my goals and values, reminding me of what truly matters to me in the long run. Over time, this practice diminished my impulsive tendencies and instilled a sense of peace.

Step 3: Establish Routine Checks

Creating a routine that includes regular check-ins with yourself helps maintain balance. Ask yourself, "How am I feeling? Do I really want a drink, or am I seeking something else?" This habitual introspection fosters a balanced approach to alcohol.

My experience: I made it a habit to conduct these check-ins during times when I would typically reach for a drink. It became a ritual that often led me to choose healthier alternatives, like a cup of coffee. And I often made it a fancy one. Treating myself to a double Café Latte with an additional shot of espresso was truly delightful, and each time, I was gratified by the sense of mastering my decisions.

Step 5: Replace Old Habits with New Ones

The nature of habits is that they can be reshaped. Identify the habitual patterns that lead to unbalanced drinking and consciously replace them with positive habits. For example, if you're used to having a drink after work to unwind, consider replacing it with a workout, a hobby, or preparing a special non-alcoholic beverage.

Habits can be stubborn and persistent, but you need to understand that it is a paradigm inside of you that require your control. Only you can do it. It is not an easy task, but it is undoubtedly achievable, solely through your efforts. This book is a very good tool to help you change stubborn habits into healthy habits.

My Experience: I was often having a glass of wine after work. I deserved it, I convinced myself – because it's been a rough day. However – once I switched to a cup of coffee or tea, my workdays felt less rough. I realized I had been deceiving myself to justify the wine.

Step 5: Practice Self-Compassion and Forgiveness

Balance is not about perfection. There will be moments of overindulgence or slips along the way. It's crucial to practice self-compassion, forgive yourself, and move forward. Each moment is a new opportunity to choose balance.

My experience: I learned to forgive myself for the times I faltered. Instead of spiraling into self-criticism,

I acknowledged the slip, explored its cause, and re-committed to my balanced drinking goals.

Integrating Balance into Your Life

The steps towards balanced alcohol consumption are not linear, but rather cyclical. They require revisiting and refining as you grow and as your relationship with alcohol evolves. Throughout this process, keep in mind that balance is an internal state, reflected in your external choices.

Conclusion:
Keep in mind that the quest for balance is a continuous one, a path that you pave with each mindful decision. In sharing these experiences and strategies, I hope to empower you to find your equilibrium and to celebrate the joys of life with or without a glass in hand. Embrace this, for it is within you that the scales of balance will find their harmony.

Navigating Social Scenes: Techniques to Avoid Overdrinking

Social gatherings are the tapestry of our lives, rich with the threads of connection and celebration. Yet, they can also be a challenging arena for those committed to mindful drinking. This chapter will guide you through navigating these social scenes, equipping you with techniques to avoid overdrinking without sacrificing your social life.

It's not about declining invitations or distancing yourself from the joy of togetherness; it's about engaging fully, with intention and strategy.

Embracing the Challenge

The first truth to embrace is that challenges and temptations will be present. Accept that they are part of the social fabric and not an indication of your failure or weakness. Your mindful drinking strategy is your compass here, not a barrier.

Technique 1: Prepare Your Strategy

Refer back to your personal drinking strategy. Prior to the event, revisit the reasons behind your choices, establish your boundaries, and clarify your goals. Developing a well-defined plan regarding the number of drinks you are comfortable consuming, or whether to abstain altogether, serves as a strong cornerstone for a successful approach to managing alcohol intake.

Share your strategy with a single trusted individual, whether it's your spouse, a close friend, or a mentor, for accountability and support. Keeping it personal by avoiding sharing with everyone ensures confidentiality and a deeper level of trust. Having a trusted confidant assist you in staying accountable to your daily or nightly strategy can be incredibly beneficial, providing motivation, feedback, and a sense of shared responsibility towards achieving your goals.

Technique 2: Have Your 'Excuse' Ready

It's unfortunate that society often expects an explanation for personal choices, but having an excuse at the ready can diffuse persistent offers of alcohol. The universal 'I'm driving tonight' is both responsible and usually respected. Other 'excuses' can include health reasons, early commitments the following day, or simply taking a break from alcohol.

You shouldn't really care about what other people think of your decision. However, I mention it in this book, because I myself was struggling in the beginning with others opinion. You will get past that point, I guarantee you. And when you do, you'll reflect on how silly it was back when you felt you had to have an "excuse".
Look at it as a transition. When your new choices kick in as a habit, you'll no longer have to use brain capacity to care of others opinion.

On the contrary you might find yourself inspiring other people. I did.

Once, my spouse and I made a conscious decision to have a six-month period without alcohol showed to be a choice that earned us respect and credibility among our peers.

During a social gathering at a friend's party, the absence of wine in our glasses sparked curiosity among the other guests, prompting questions about our abstinence. Some wondering others admiring.

My attention was drawn to a fellow guest who, unfortunately had a few too many. I was sharp as a razer and could silently observe all the details in his behavior.

Reflecting on this scene, I refrained from passing judgment, instead choosing to introspect about my own past encounters with alcohol and reaffirming my commitment to a healthier and more fulfilling lifestyle.

A curious friend delved into our motives and the positive impact of our alcohol-free lifestyle.

As we shared the benefits such as enhanced sleep quality, physical well-being, and mental sharpness, our friend felt inspired to kickstart a similar journey right then and there. He even got his wife on board and later on, they told us how grateful they were for the decision as they have experienced the same benefits and a body and mind thanking them for the attention.

There will always be people who will judge your decisions – don't worry about that. It's inside them – not you.

Technique 3: Be the First to Order

Take control of the situation by being proactive and taking the lead in ordering drinks.

Consider ordering a non-alcoholic beverage or selecting a drink that resonates with your overall strategy for the occasion. This initial choice sets the tone for your drinking habits throughout the event.

Moreover, your decision could serve as an inspiration to those around you, influencing them positively with your thoughtful selection.

Whenever I am out dining on a restaurant with friends, I often find myself being the first to order sparkling water. This was not how it used to be. This habit has now become ingrained, establishing a new standard for the entire circle of friends. No one ever asks or wonder anymore.

Technique 4: Offer to Be the Designated Driver

By offering to be the designated driver, you assume a role that not only justifies your choice not to drink but is also valued and respected by others. Being the designated driver not only ensures everyone's safety but also contributes to a positive and responsible social environment.

This act of responsibility can lead to meaningful conversations and connections with friends and acquaintances. Additionally, this role can offer a sense of purpose that transcends the event itself, fostering a deeper sense of fulfillment and satisfaction.

Technique 5: Embrace Alternative Pleasures

When attending an event your old paradigm or habit will probably encourage you to drink. To restrain from that "old you" to set the scene, you can make sure that you are engaged in other activities.

Indulge in the various delights and experiences the event has to offer – lose yourself in the rhythm of the music, participate in entertaining activities, relish the diverse and delicious cuisine, and engage in stimulating and enriching conversations.

There can be a whole new world opening for you, by immersing yourself in the multifaceted encounters the event presents, rather than focusing solely on alcohol consumption.

Technique 6: Optical Illusions

When attending social gatherings, and your strategy is to skip alcohol after the dinner or even the entire night, virgin drinks are always a really good alternative. By making this choice, you can still savor the experience with a beverage in hand, be it a mocktail or a refreshing soda.

Explore a variety of cocktails to discover your preferences. Whether you enjoy fruity and refreshing mixes or prefer the classic elegance of a martini, there's always a non-alcoholic option available to suit your taste.

Trust me, the world of virgin drinks is filled with surprisingly delicious options waiting to be explored.

If you haven't tried one yet, you might be pleasantly surprised by the burst of flavors and creativity in these alcohol-free concoctions.

Temptation, honesty and internal struggles

You are up against our own habits and desires, and that is very common when it comes to drinking. But with a strong strategy in place, and the support of trusted individuals, you can overcome these challenges and find alternative pleasures that bring more joy and fulfillment into your life. Remember, change is not easy, but it is within your power. Stay motivated, stay committed, and stay true to yourself.

When faced with temptation, take a moment to pause and remind yourself of your goals. Recall the reasons why you're on this path and the progress you've made. Let these reflections reinforce your resolve. Face your temptation with grace – not fear. Overcoming that first temptation, will give you a big win. It will motivate you to keep going. Ride that wave.

Be honest about it. If you're comfortable about your Mindful Drinking it will show, and you'll be respected by others.

On the contrary, if you're uneasy, others will pick up on it, making it tougher to decline. So be confident in your choices and stand by them. Your well-being is worth it.
It will cause internal struggles; you will have wins and you will have failures.

Feel the struggles without fear (they are here for a reason), embrace and celebrate the wins and learn from your failures.

After experiencing a setback, a friend offered me wisdom that has since resonated with me: "It is what it is. Take the best from it and forgive the rest", he said. This advice has stayed with me, reinforcing the idea that there is always a lesson to be learned. Each experience, regardless of its nature, holds value as long as we apply the knowledge gained.

And to end this chapter, I'd like to share some other thoughts on failure shared by the late and great Bob Proctor. Keep that in mind when you fail. Because you will. But you'll get right back up.

" The way to succeed is to double your failure rate. Of course, failure is never desirable, but it is inevitable, and with a proper attitude, it can be quite useful. ", Bob Proctor.

Building a Healthy Long Term Alcohol Friendship

Alcohol, like any friend, can bring joy into our lives, enrich experiences, and accompany us through both celebrations and challenges. But as with any relationship, the one we foster with alcohol requires care, respect, and boundaries. This chapter guides you on the path to building a friendship with alcohol that is healthy, sustainable, and life-enhancing, echoing the principles laid out in previous chapters.

In our journey together through this book, we've established the foundation of mindful drinking. From recognizing early warning signs to crafting a personal drinking strategy, each step has been about fostering self-awareness and intentionality. It's important to recall these lessons because they form the bedrock of a healthy long-term relationship with alcohol.

Recall the "Five Steps Towards Balanced Alcohol Consumption" we explored in Chapter 5. Balance does not occur overnight—it's an art, a steady practice of mindful choices and checks. Maintaining this balance is an ongoing process that calls for daily attention and care, much like a garden that needs tending to thrive.

The Mindful Circle of Friendship

Just as we choose our friends wisely, we must be discerning about our relationship with alcohol. Ask yourself: does it uplift me? Does it align with my values and contribute positively to my life? These questions, stemming from the self-reflection techniques shared in earlier chapters, are crucial to assess continually.

Seeing your relationship with alcohol as a friend and comparing it to a friendship with a dear person, can help your perspective.

Always treat a friend with respect and always expect respect in return. If your friend – or alcohol – doesn't treat you with respect as a friend should, cut it out of your life. It doesn't deserve you. And you are much better of without it.

Overcoming Setbacks. A Guide to Resilience

Setbacks are not merely roadblocks encountered on your journey; they serve as guideposts signaling a crucial need for reflection, thoughtful adjustment, and a revitalized commitment to progress.

Stay true to your path, and let resilience be your ally in navigating through setbacks as you redefine your relationship with alcohol. Keep learning, keep growing, and keep moving forward on this transformative journey towards a more mindful relationship with alcohol.

This is a deeply personal and arduous process of reshaping your relationship with alcohol, and it is important to delve into the inherent inevitability of setbacks and, more significantly, illuminate the strategies to gracefully navigate through them, ensuring you remain steadfast on your path towards mindful drinking and personal growth.

Your success is within reach – stay resilient!

Setbacks are an integral part of any transformative process. They are not indications of failure but are, in fact, opportunities for learning and growth.

As we have established in earlier chapters, the path to a mindful relationship with alcohol is not linear. It is woven with complexities, such as moments of self-reflection, understanding triggers, and building resilience. Unexpected turns in this journey can sometimes lead us astray, but they also offer valuable lessons that contribute to our personal growth and development.

Do not get upset with yourself and viewing yourself as a failure. This mindset is unproductive and hinders your ability to realign and move forward. Remember, setbacks are a natural part of growth and change. Approach them with compassion, curiosity, and determination. Keep pushing forward, one step at a time.

When faced with a setback, it is natural to feel vulnerable. Embrace this feeling. Vulnerability is a powerful teacher that shows us where our strategies need fortification. It reminds us of the 'why' behind our commitment to change, which is a profound motivator to push forward.

Circling back to your strategy

Your personal drinking strategy is your anchor during times of setback. It's a blueprint that guides you back to your intended course. Revisit it, reflect upon it, and remember that it was crafted to serve as a compass during precisely these challenging times. Utilize the tools and support system mentioned earlier to help you stay on track. Remember, every setback is an opportunity for growth and learning. Keep taking small steps forward, practicing self-compassion, and staying committed to your journey towards mindful drinking.

Every setback you encounter in life serves as a repository of valuable wisdom waiting to be unearthed. Instead of approaching it with self-criticism, greet it with curiosity, delving into the depths of its origins. What were the triggers that led to this obstacle? How did you react in the face of adversity? What lessons can be learned from this experience? These contemplations not only aid in comprehending the setback but also equip you with insights to navigate and potentially prevent similar challenges in the future.

This will also emphasize the importance of having a strategy. You will discover, that if you are not true to your strategy, then you will fail. So, remind yourself of your strategy and focus on sticking to it.

Journaling

Consider keeping a journal during setbacks. By tracking what caused your failures, you'll notice patterns over time. These recurring situations are likely the culprits. Recognizing them will empower you to sidestep such pitfalls more effectively.

Seeing the pattern makes you able use them as opportunities to learn and grow. Stay resilient, stay committed, and always remember the reasons behind your journey towards a healthier relationship with alcohol. Your future self will thank you for it.

Use this journal to document not just the setback, but your response to it. How did you and your surroundings respond? This practice can become a source of encouragement, as it catalogues the challenges AND your capacity to overcome them.

Journal your way back on track. Your way back to the strategy. If necessary, adjust your strategy to avoid the pitfalls that you have experienced to set you off track.

Keeping a journal of setbacks, documenting your reactions, thoughts, and how you get back on track, can reduce self-blame when facing future challenges.

Blaming yourself is not your friend, in fact it is an enemy you don't want to have.

Self-compassion is a non-negotiable companion. Be kind to yourself. Acknowledge the effort it takes to confront and rise above setbacks. Self-compassion is the balm that heals the wounds of setbacks and strengthens your resolve to move forward.

Lastly, view each setback as a steppingstone to a future where your relationship with alcohol is not defined by the obstacles you've faced, but by the resilience you've shown in overcoming them. There will always be challenges, but within you lies an indomitable spirit, capable of rising, time and again, to steer you back to the path of mindful drinking.

You've got this!

9. Attitude of Gratitude

Having read this far, hopefully you are inspired to a new life that embraces Mindful Drinking. It is my hope that you feel the stirrings of a renewed life, a life of balance and awareness. Take a moment to be grateful. Grateful for taking the decision to live a better life.

You have a lot to be grateful for. Shift your perspective to one of gratitude. Let it become the new standard for you. Adopt an Attitude of Gratitude.

Be grateful for the small things happening to you. Even things you didn't pay attention to before. The extra kindness of somebody, the warmth of sunlight on your skin, a stranger's spontaneous smile, the infectious laughter of children, or the serene song of birds at dawn.

Embrace gratitude not just as an occasional guest in your thoughts but as a constant, vibrant companion. This shift in attitude lays the foundation for a life where every moment is an opportunity for thankfulness, propelling you towards lasting change and a heartening journey with mindful drinking.

And with an Attitude of Gratitude, you'll see the whole world around you in another perspective, and you will be confirmed that life must be lived to the fullest, which is fuel to your journey to a balanced life with a healthy relationship with alcohol.

I know you can do it. You know it, too. And what awaits you is worth it all, and you'll thank yourself for the rest of your life. I'm cheering for you.

Beyond the book; Continuing Your Journey

As we arrive at the end of this book, I offer you a piece of advice—arguably the most profound I've ever received.

My therapist that asked me once: "What version of you would you like to be when you get older?" At first, I was uncertain of the meaning and how to respond. However, upon reflection, I recognized its significance. This question, perhaps the most critical one can contemplate, invites profound self-reflection and foresight into one's future self.

Defining your **"Future Self"**is a very powerful exercise and I strongly recommend you put some effort into it. This enables you to engage with that envisioned "self," allowing for meaningful discussions, inquiries, and reflections.

My advice is to personify your future self, maybe even name that version of yourself.

To encourage you to shape your future self, I will share my own Future Self with you. It is very personal, but since you made it to the end of this book, you deserve it.

Back to the question: *"What version of you would you like to be when you get older?"*
Essentially the question is about WHO do you really want to be?

I thought deeply about it, and here is who I really want to be, and who I will be (my Future Self)

I am a powerful woman who leads by example, embodying and promoting kindness, and always giving more than I expect to receive. I serve as an inspiration to others, guiding and uplifting them on their journey to fulfillment. I am respected for my actions, which always stem from a place of gratitude and unconditional love.

This holds so many values to me, and there is no way that my Future Self can be an alcoholic, or even have a troubled relationship with alcohol.

I call this version of myself: "Future Me" or sometimes "Greater Me."

Whenever I face a dilemma, I contemplate, "How would my **Greater Me** tackle this?" This approach applies to all challenges, not just those related to alcohol.

How would you describe your Future Self? Take a moment to really think and write it down. You can refine it over time, but make sure it aligns with who you really want to be.

Now, you have recognized and defined who you truly aspire to be, which is an admirable achievement. Engage in dialogue with your Future Self, envision the life you wish and most crucially, embody your future self in your daily life.

Let your Future Self guide you from here.

By defining your Future Self and constantly working towards embodying that vision, you will find fulfillment and purpose in your life. Trust in yourself, believe in your potential, and always strive to be the best version of yourself - your Future Self.

The path that lies beyond this book is your personal journey, characterized by the ongoing development of your character and the choices you make. Your future self is not an elusive dream but rather a reality currently in progress.

Keep the vision of who you aspire to be close to your heart, refer to it frequently, and move forward with the assurance that each day presents a chance to manifest that vision into reality. Remember, you are the artisan of your fate, molding the present into the masterpiece of your future.

So, go forth with confidence and conviction, knowing that you are in control of your life and the choices you make shape your destiny. Let your Future Self guide you towards a fulfilling and purposeful life. Keep asking yourself - would my Future Self be proud of me?

Remember with determination and consistency, you can achieve anything you set your mind to. Remember to be patient and kind to yourself along the way.

And lastly, always remember that self-care is a necessary component of personal growth. Take time for yourself, whether it be through mindfulness practices, hobbies, or simply enjoying some quiet time alone. This will not only recharge and refresh your mind, but it will also allow you to reflect on your progress and continue moving towards your Future Self.

Remember, you are the sculptor of your destiny, shaping the clay of today into the masterpiece of tomorrow.

Made in the USA
Las Vegas, NV
05 January 2025